# Who Was
# Franklin Roosevelt?

# Who Was
# Franklin Roosevelt?

By Margaret Frith
Illustrated by John O'Brien

Grosset & Dunlap
An Imprint of Penguin Group (USA) Inc.

For my American Mother—M.F.
For Terase—J.O.

GROSSET & DUNLAP
Published by the Penguin Group
Penguin Group (USA) Inc., 375 Hudson Street, New York, New York 10014, USA
Penguin Group (Canada), 90 Eglinton Avenue East, Suite 700,
Toronto, Ontario M4P 2Y3, Canada
(a division of Pearson Penguin Canada Inc.)
Penguin Books Ltd., 80 Strand, London WC2R 0RL, England
Penguin Group Ireland, 25 St. Stephen's Green, Dublin 2, Ireland
(a division of Penguin Books Ltd.)
Penguin Group (Australia), 250 Camberwell Road, Camberwell, Victoria 3124, Australia
(a division of Pearson Australia Group Pty. Ltd.)
Penguin Books India Pvt. Ltd., 11 Community Centre,
Panchsheel Park, New Delhi—110 017, India
Penguin Group (NZ), 67 Apollo Drive, Rosedale, North Shore 0632, New Zealand
(a division of Pearson New Zealand Ltd.)
Penguin Books (South Africa) (Pty.) Ltd., 24 Sturdee Avenue,
Rosebank, Johannesburg 2196, South Africa

Penguin Books Ltd., Registered Offices:
80 Strand, London WC2R 0RL, England

Text copyright © 2010 by Margaret Frith. Interior illustrations copyright © 2010 by
John O'Brien. Cover illustration copyright © 2010 by Nancy Harrison. All rights
reserved. Published by Grosset & Dunlap, a division of Penguin Young Readers Group,
345 Hudson Street, New York, New York 10014. GROSSET & DUNLAP is
a trademark of Penguin Group (USA) Inc. Printed in the U.S.A.

Library of Congress Cataloging-in-Publication Data

Frith, Margaret.
Who was Franklin Roosevelt? / by Margaret Frith ; Illustrated by John O'Brien.
p. cm.
ISBN 978-0-448-45346-0 (pbk.)
1. Roosevelt, Franklin D. (Franklin Delano), 1882-1945--Juvenile literature.
2. Presidents--United States--Biography--Juvenile literature. I. O'Brien, John, 1953- ill.
II. Title.
E807.F78 2010
973.917092--dc22
[B]

2009023143

ISBN 978-0-448-45346-0        10 9 8 7 6 5 4

# Contents

# Who Was
# Franklin Delano Roosevelt?

When Franklin Delano Roosevelt died in 1945, a young soldier stood in front of the White House remembering his president. "I felt as if I knew him. I felt as if he knew me—and I felt as if he liked me." He was saying what so many Americans were feeling.

FDR, as he was called, had been president since 1933. He was elected four times, serving for twelve years. This was longer than any other president before or since.

When Franklin took office, there were lots of problems waiting for him. Banks were failing. People were out of work. Many had lost their homes. This was the Great Depression.

Franklin wasn't a man to sit around and wonder what to do. In the first hundred days, he signed fifteen major laws bringing help. No president had ever gotten so much done so fast.

Franklin not only dealt with the Depression, he led the country through the dark days of World War II.

What made him such a strong leader? Perhaps his strength came in part from a personal crisis. It happened when he was thirty-nine years old. He was on summer vacation with his family. Overnight he was struck with a disease called *polio*. Franklin never walked again. But he fought hard to stay strong and healthy. He never gave up. He ran the country with the same spirit and optimism.

Not everyone liked Franklin's ideas. But most of the country loved him. Millions wept as if he were part of their family when they learned of his sudden death. Many could not imagine the United States without FDR as president.

# Chapter 1
# Growing Up in Hyde Park

SPRINGWOOD

In a big house called Springwood, high above the Hudson River in Hyde Park, New York, a baby boy was born on January 30, 1882.

"At a quarter to nine my Sallie had a splendid large baby boy. He weighs ten pounds without clothes," his father, James Roosevelt, wrote. The baby's mother, Sara Delano Roosevelt, said that he was "pink, plump and nice." She named him Franklin after her favorite uncle.

When they met, Sara was twenty-five and
James was fifty-one, a widower with a grown son.
James fell in love with Sara at a dinner party. The
hostess remembered that James couldn't keep his
eyes off Sara. They were married in 1880.

Sara and James came from old, wealthy
families in the Hudson Valley. They grew up in
lovely homes with lots of help—cooks, butlers,
maids, and gardeners. James was a gentleman
farmer and hired workers to do the farming.

Franklin was an only child. He was the apple of his mother's eye and Franklin loved her very much, even when she was bossy.

Franklin grew up around adults. He did not go to school. He was taught at home by tutors until he was thirteen. Yet, even with no other

children around, Franklin found life at Springwood fun. In the winter, he went on sleigh rides or sledded full speed down snowy hills. He was happy exploring the woods and fields. Franklin loved horseback riding with Popsy. That's what he called his father.

From an early age, Franklin began collecting stamps. This was a hobby he enjoyed all his life. His greatest love, however, was the sea. He played with model boats. He sailed in the summer. And when he was older, he went iceboating on the Hudson River in the bitter cold. (An iceboat was like a sled with sails and went very fast.)

When Franklin was nine, Popsy bought a
yacht called the *Half Moon*. Franklin was excited
to go sailing on it at Campobello.

Campobello is an island off the east coast of Canada. The Roosevelts spent summers there in a cottage they had built. The strong winds and high tides made sailing around the island tricky. But Franklin loved the challenge and became a fine sailor. At sixteen, he had his own sailboat, *New Moon*.

Another family on Campobello told the Roosevelts about the Groton School. It was a boarding school north of Boston, Massachusetts. Franklin's parents decided to send him there.

Most of the boys started at Groton when they were twelve. But Franklin didn't go until he was fourteen. His mother couldn't bear to let him go earlier. Not surprisingly, he was homesick at first.

Life at Groton was very different from Springwood. It was modeled after an English boarding school with no frills and a harsh lifestyle. Franklin lived in a room with other boys. Once, during the night, snow blew in through an open transom of the dorm. Franklin and the boys woke up nearly freezing. Still, that didn't excuse them from the cold shower they had to take every morning.

Sports were important at Groton, and to Franklin. He loved playing football. He was slight and not very fast. Still, he fought hard and had the scrapes and bumps to prove it.

His parents were more interested in his studies. It pleased them that he was fourth in his class of nineteen boys.

## HARVARD YARD

In the spring of 1900, Franklin graduated from Groton. That fall, he entered Harvard. For the past few years, his father's health had been failing. Soon after Thanksgiving, Franklin got word that Popsy was very ill. He died of heart failure on December 8.

Now Sara was a widow. Rather than spend the winter in Hyde Park alone, she moved to Boston to be near Franklin. Already close, mother and son grew even closer.

At Harvard, Franklin became a great success on the *Crimson*, the college newspaper. He was a natural writer with a knack for good interviews. His senior year, he was president of the *Crimson*. But the most significant thing that happened during his Harvard years was his friendship with his distant cousin Eleanor Roosevelt.

# Chapter 2
# Meeting Eleanor

Unlike Franklin, Eleanor had an unhappy childhood. Her father was the younger brother of Theodore Roosevelt, who became president in 1901. Elliott was handsome and engaging.

Eleanor adored him and he adored his little
daughter. But he had a bad drinking problem.
Her mother, Anna Hall Roosevelt, was a cold
and distant mother. She called Eleanor "Granny"
because she was such a serious child. Eleanor
felt like an awkward ugly duckling next to her
beautiful mother.

Both of Eleanor's parents and her younger brother had all died by the time she was ten. So she and her six-year-old brother, Hall, were sent to live with their grandparents. The Halls found it a burden to have two young children come to live with them.

Often lonely, Eleanor would escape into dreams of happy times with her father. One bright spot was Christmastime when she would see her Roosevelt cousins at parties.

Franklin was at one of these parties. He asked her to dance. She accepted even though she didn't know how. It didn't seem to matter to Franklin.

After that, they didn't see each other again for several years. Eleanor went off to boarding school in England. (She said later that these were "the happiest years of her life.")

At eighteen, she returned to America. As a young girl from a famous family, it was time for her to take her place in New York society. She said she was in "utter agony."

But she saw Franklin again at the parties. When he invited her to his twenty-first birthday party at Springwood, she went. Gradually they began seeing more of each other. He was fun and he made her laugh.

Franklin's mother didn't want her son to get serious about any girl. She wanted him to finish college and start a career. Yet Franklin grew fonder and fonder of Eleanor. She was smart and more interesting than other girls. She had lived and traveled in Europe. She spoke French even better than he did. And with her tall, slim figure, gold hair that fell below her waist, and lovely blue eyes, she was not an "ugly duckling." Not in his eyes.

Franklin asked Eleanor to marry him and she said yes. Sara was not at all pleased with the news. But she stayed calm and asked them not to rush into marriage. They were too young. So Franklin and Eleanor agreed to wait. Sara whisked her son off on a six-week cruise to the Caribbean. Secretly she hoped he might forget Eleanor. Instead, the trip made him long to get back to her.

Finally, in the fall of 1904, Sara gave in and
they announced their engagement. Franklin
and Eleanor were married in New York City
on March 17, 1905. Eleanor's uncle Ted, the
president, gave away the bride.

After a three-month honeymoon, the couple returned to New York City. Sara had taken care of everything, leaving Eleanor with nothing to do. They moved into a home completely furnished and only three blocks from where Sara lived in New York. (A few years later, Sara would build two buildings next to each other with connecting doors on different floors that were never locked. It was almost like living together.)

The couple's first child, Anna Eleanor, was born in 1906. James was born a year later. Sadly, their third child, Franklin, would die of the flu

when he was only eight months old. They would have three more children—Elliott, Franklin Jr., and John.

Franklin studied at Columbia Law School just as Eleanor's uncle Ted had. Then he joined a well-known law firm on Wall Street. However, the job never really excited him. And, although he loved Hyde Park, Franklin did not want to spend his life as a gentleman farmer like his father.

What did appeal to him? Politics! So, in 1910, Franklin ran for office. He was twenty-eight years old.

# Chapter 3
# Running for Office

Important Democrats in the Hyde Park area asked Franklin to run for the New York Senate.

If he won, he would work in Albany, the state capital. With a famous last name and the money to pay for his own campaign, Franklin seemed like a good candidate, even though most of the voters in the district were Republicans.

But he knew that the Roosevelt name wasn't enough. He needed voters to get to know him.

So he hired a large, flashy, red automobile and asked a popular congressman to travel with him. Off they went in high spirits, flags flying, the wind in their faces.

People enjoyed meeting this friendly young man who talked about honest government. On election day, he defeated his opponent by 1,440 votes. He spent three years in the state senate and became known for being independent. He was not someone who did what the party bosses

LOUIS HOWE

told him. It was also during this time that he met a newspaperman named Louis Howe. Howe became a lifelong friend and aide.

In 1912, Franklin attended the Democratic Convention in Baltimore, Maryland. He was backing Governor Woodrow Wilson from New Jersey for president. Wilson won the nomination and went on to win the election in November.

Franklin had supported Wilson not only because of his ideas, but also because he hoped to land a job in Washington. That happened

WOODROW WILSON

almost right way! Franklin was asked if he would like to become Assistant Secretary of the Navy.

"How would I like it? I'd like it bully well," he answered.

With his love of the sea and sailing, the navy was just the right place for Franklin. He wanted to learn all he could about the navy. He talked to everyone from admirals to sailors to builders in the yards. He visited naval stations around the

country. It was not unusual to see him climbing up the rigging of a ship as it plowed through the waves. Even top admirals came to respect this young man who had never been in the navy himself.

In 1914, World War I broke out in Europe. In 1917, the United States joined forces against Germany.

Franklin urged the navy to build powerful battleships.

It was a proud day when he hammered the first bolt into a brand-new battleship in the Brooklyn Navy Yard. It was named the USS *Arizona*.

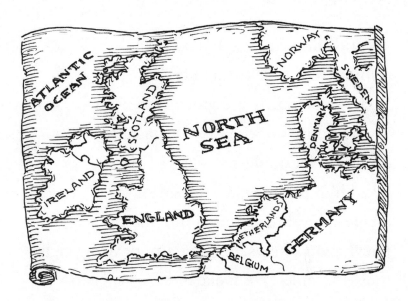

He also had a sharp understanding of warfare. Franklin convinced the navy to lay a belt of underwater mines in the North Sea. German submarines had to pass through this area to get to the Atlantic Ocean in order to attack British and American ships. It was late in the war, but by blowing up German subs, the mines kept the ships safer.

The war ended on November 11, 1918, with Germany's defeat. Franklin was sent to Paris to attend the peace treaty conference.

With the war over, Franklin was
ready to return to private life. It was
1920—a presidential election year.
To Franklin's surprise, the Democratic
candidate for president—James Cox—
asked him to run as vice president.

Franklin threw himself into the campaign.
He visited twenty states by train, traveling eight
thousand miles. He spoke to farmers, factory
workers, city workers, businessmen, and women
who were voting for the first time.

Franklin and Cox weren't expected to win and they didn't. In fact, they lost badly. But Franklin loved the race. All across the country, people got to know this sunny, optimistic man from New York who seemed to have a great future ahead of him.

## Chapter 4
## Facing a Crisis

In 1921, Franklin was back in New York working as a lawyer. That August, he joined Eleanor and the children at their cottage on Campobello.

One morning, when the family was out sailing, they saw smoke rising from a small island. They sailed over and found a brushfire out of control. Franklin cut evergreen branches and they beat at the flames for hours. Finally, they got the fire out.

Back on Campobello, Franklin and his sons went for a swim. Then Franklin sat around in his wet bathing suit looking at the mail. He felt cold and his back ached, so he went to bed early. The next day, he woke up and could hardly stand.

Eleanor called a doctor. He thought Franklin had a cold. But as the days went by, Franklin grew worse. He couldn't get out of bed. His whole body ached. He was in terrible pain.

Another doctor came. He said the same thing. Franklin had a bad cold. Finally, Eleanor had a doctor from Boston come down and examine Franklin.

He knew immediately what was wrong. Franklin had polio. Polio was a virus that caused high fevers and often left people unable to walk.

Eleanor took Franklin home to New York. If he felt scared or worried, he didn't let on. Right away, he started exercising at home. He was determined to walk again.

In February, Franklin got steel braces for his legs. They were attached to leather belts around his hips and chest. When the hinges at his knees were locked, he was able to stand but not walk. (Later, when he was president, he had his braces painted black. He wore them with black shoes and socks so they wouldn't be noticed.)

Sara convinced Franklin that he would
be more comfortable at Springwood.
So the family moved to Hyde Park. It
was hard for Eleanor. Once again, her
mother-in-law was in charge.

The bedrooms at Springwood were
on the second floor. There was no way
Franklin could use the stairs. Luckily the
house had a "trunk lift" for luggage. It was
the size of an elevator, so Franklin could fit
in it in his wheelchair. It was hauled up and
down with ropes
and pulleys.

Franklin tried
anything he heard
about that might
help his legs—
sunlamps, electric
belts, massages,
and pulleys.

Once, he even tried hanging from the ceiling by a
harness. Nothing worked. He couldn't walk and
he was no nearer walking with crutches.

Still, he made a wonderful discovery.
Swimming. He could float without any help.
He was sure it was helping his legs.

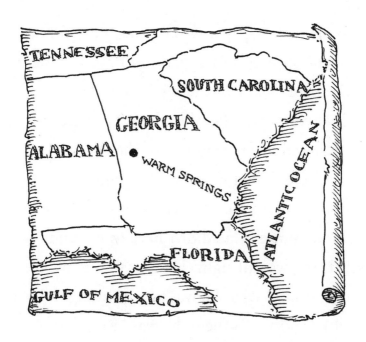

In 1924, Franklin heard about a place with "miracle waters." It was called Warm Springs and it was in the backwoods of Georgia. He and Eleanor needed a vacation so they went.

There was an old hotel, twelve run-down cottages, and a swimming pool. The minute Franklin got in, he beamed. The water was ninety degrees. "How marvelous it feels," he said. "I don't think I'll ever get out."

When a newspaper wrote about Franklin's stay at Warm Springs, other victims of polio started going there. Many of them were children.

Two years later, Franklin bought the resort and restored it. He kept one of the cottages for himself. He visited whenever he could.

Franklin had found a second home. Here he could be himself. He didn't have to pretend everything was all right. He was among people going through what he was going through. They loved Franklin. To them, he was "Rosy."

He had wonderful, boisterous times with the children. Loud laughter and splashing meant that Franklin and the children were playing water games in the pool.

In 1927, Franklin started the Georgia Warm Springs Foundation. It treated victims of polio and became a center for studying the disease.

As for Franklin, he was learning to live fully despite his crippled legs. His car was adapted so

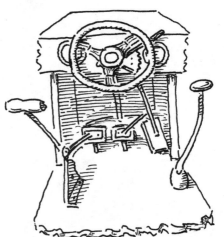

VIEW OF HAND CONTROLS
THIS MADE DRIVING POSSIBLE
WITHOUT USING FEET.

that he could drive using only his hands. He still loved to drive fast. He flew down the roads, stopping to talk to anyone along the way.

It was on these trips around Georgia that Franklin became aware of what it meant to be poor and struggling—to live without electricity or go to a rundown school. He never forgot what he saw.

# POLIO

SOME VICTIMS OF POLIO RECOVERED WITH LITTLE OR NO DAMAGE. BUT MANY, LIKE FRANKLIN, WERE NOT SO LUCKY.

MOST POLIO OUTBREAKS OCCURRED IN THE SUMMER. IN THE EPIDEMIC OF 1916, SIX THOUSAND PEOPLE DIED. THE WORST YEAR WAS IN 1952 WHEN THERE WERE OVER FIFTY-SEVEN THOUSAND CASES.

IN 1938, PRESIDENT ROOSEVELT FOUNDED THE MARCH OF DIMES FOR POLIO RESEARCH. EVERYONE WAS ASKED TO SEND IN A DIME.

IN 1955, DR. JONAS SALK CAME UP WITH THE FIRST VACCINE TO PREVENT POLIO. SINCE THAT TIME, POLIO HAS BEEN ELIMINATED IN MOST OF THE WORLD. IT IS TOO BAD FRANKLIN DID NOT LIVE TO SEE A POLIO VACCINE.

AFTER HIS DEATH, HIS PORTRAIT WAS PUT ON THE DIME. HIS PORTRAIT STILL APPEARS ON IT, IN MEMORY OF HIS WORK FOR THE MARCH OF DIMES.

# Chapter 5
# Struggling to Walk

Franklin was determined to run for office again one day. But he wanted to walk first. It was important for the Democratic Party to remember him. So he kept in touch through letters and phone calls.

Eleanor was determined to keep Franklin's name alive. "I don't want him forgotten," she said. "I want him to have a voice." Louis Howe convinced her to attend political meetings. He coached her on how to speak in public. She began to enjoy a political life of her own. Women's causes were important to her.

Although Franklin worked as hard as he could, he still couldn't walk. But he came up with a way of standing and moving forward, swinging one leg, then the other. He would hold tightly to the arm of a person on one side and use a crutch on the other. Eventually he could lean on a cane instead of a crutch. It wasn't walking, but he made it look like walking.

In 1924, the Democratic Party asked Franklin to nominate Al Smith, the Governor of New York, to run for president. The convention was held in Madison Square Garden in New York City.

Franklin wanted to appear strong and confident. He got to the podium with the help of a crutch and his son James. It was a great struggle, but Franklin made it with sweat pouring down

AL SMITH

his face. He gripped the podium and stood
straight and tall. His face lit up with a big smile
and the crowd went wild.

By now, he must have known that he would never walk again. But a life in politics was certainly possible. And when the time came to campaign, he would face the American people, standing tall.

Four years later, in 1928, Roosevelt was elected governor of New York. He won by only twenty-five thousand votes out of more than four million cast. Still, he won.

Republicans were in charge of the state government. At his opening address, Franklin was charming and cheerful. He spoke of new laws to protect workers and unions. But the Republicans were not interested in hearing about these issues.

Then, in October 1929, the unexpected happened. The stock market on Wall Street crashed and the country turned upside down. People lost their money. Then they lost their jobs.

This was the beginning of the Great Depression.

By 1932, at least twelve million men and
women were out of work. They lined up at soup

kitchens for free food. Many lost their homes and
had nowhere to live. With only the clothes on

their backs, they gathered in "squatter camps"—
sometimes called *Hoovervilles* after the president
Herbert Hoover.

Franklin was convinced that now was the time
to run for president. He campaigned across the
country on the "Roosevelt Special." At every stop,

this tall, attractive, confident man stood and promised to get people back to work. He offered them a future.

HERBERT HOOVER

Americans listened and saw a leader they could count on.

Franklin beat his opponent, President Herbert Hoover, by a landslide. Out of forty-eight states, he lost only six.

The Roosevelt era had begun.

# Chapter 6
# Becoming President

Franklin's campaign song had been "Happy Days Are Here Again." After he was sworn in as the thirty-second president of the United States,

Franklin spoke to the nation. He promised them: "Action and action now." He was going to start new programs to help them. He said, "The only thing we have to fear is fear itself."

People were certainly afraid. They no longer trusted banks to keep their money safe. So they lined up to take out their savings. Without money, banks were collapsing all over the country.

Immediately, Franklin declared a four-day bank holiday. No one could take out money because banks were closed. Franklin hoped this "time-out" would calm people down. The holiday worked, but Franklin had no way of knowing that beforehand.

All his life, Franklin was willing to experiment. If he tried something and it didn't work, he would try something else. He wanted to hear ideas and opinions from lots of people. "Above all, try something."

Franklin gave his first "fireside chat" on the radio. He wanted everyone to understand what he was doing to fix the banks. "It is safer for you to keep your money in a reopened bank than to keep it under the mattress," he told them.

The White House received thousands of letters and telegrams. The fireside chat was a huge success. The president had spoken to people as a friend. They felt he cared about their problems.

# FIRESIDE CHATS ON THE RADIO

IN THE YEARS THAT FRANKLIN WAS PRESIDENT, HE HELD THIRTY-ONE OF HIS FAMOUS "FIRESIDE CHATS." THEY ALLOWED FRANKLIN TO EXPLAIN WHAT THE GOVERNMENT WAS DOING AND WHY. HE WANTED TO REACH AS MANY PEOPLE AS POSSIBLE. HIS TALKS WERE USUALLY BROADCAST ON SUNDAY EVENINGS AT NINE O'CLOCK WHEN MOST AMERICANS LISTENED TO THE RADIO.

FDR WOULD BEGIN BY SAYING, ". . . I WANT TO TALK FOR A FEW MINUTES WITH THE PEOPLE OF THE UNITED STATES . . ."

HE WORKED HARD ON WHAT HE SAID AND HOW HE WOULD SAY IT. "I'LL JUST THINK OUT LOUD," HE WOULD TELL HIS SECRETARY, "AND YOU WRITE IT DOWN." DURING A FIRESIDE CHAT, FRANKLIN HAD PEOPLE SITTING IN THE ROOM WITH HIM. HE COULD LOOK AT THEM AND IMAGINE AMERICANS ALL ACROSS THE COUNTRY LISTENING TO HIM ON THE RADIO. AND, INDEED, THEY FELT AS IF FRANKLIN WAS RIGHT IN THEIR HOMES TALKING DIRECTLY TO THEM, AS A FRIEND.

ONE TIME HE HEARD A WHISTLING SOUND COMING THROUGH A GAP BETWEEN HIS FRONT TEETH. HE DIDN'T LIKE IT, SO HE HAD A SPECIAL BRIDGE MADE JUST FOR HIS "FIRESIDE CHATS."

In the first hundred days, Congress passed fifteen major laws to help people get back to work. The programs Franklin had promised were getting underway. They became known across the country as the "New Deal."

He started many new agencies to get working on solutions.

The CCC sent young, out-of-work men to national parks and forests to plant trees, build fire stations, and put out fires.

The AAA helped farmers unable to sell their crops or pay their rent or mortgages.

The WPA built roads, hospitals, schools, and other public buildings. Artists, writers, and musicians were asked to paint murals in public buildings, write books, and perform in concerts around the country.

The NRA drew

up rules to help businesses and workers get along. Rules for prices, wages, and hours of work were set and workers could join unions to bargain with companies.

The TVA brought electricity and other improvements to rural areas in seven southern states. Franklin hadn't forgotten all those people in Georgia living without electricity.

More programs were added later. An important one that still exists today is the SSA created in 1935. The government mailed checks to retired people over sixty-five, the disabled, the unemployed, and needy children. The government got the money from workers' payroll taxes and company taxes.

These new programs cost the government a lot of money. Some people said too much money.

And they didn't like the government running things that they thought should be done by private companies. They didn't like paying higher taxes, either. But these were unusual times. Franklin was sure he was doing the right thing. And the voters thought so, too.

In 1936, Franklin ran again. He won in an even bigger landslide. This time he only lost two states, Maine and Vermont.

# TURN ON THE LIGHTS!

THE TENNESSEE VALLEY AUTHORITY (TVA)
IMPROVED THE LIVES OF POOR FAMILIES IN THE
SOUTH IN MANY WAYS. IT HELPED FARMERS GROW
BETTER CROPS. IT BUILT FACTORIES THAT CREATED
THOUSANDS OF JOBS. IT BROUGHT ELECTRICITY
INTO THE HOMES OF PEOPLE WHO, UNTIL THEN,
HAD TO DEPEND ON CANDLELIGHT OR GASLIGHT.
THIS WAS MADE POSSIBLE BY GIANT DAMS THAT
PROVIDED HYDROELECTRIC POWER TO SEVEN TVA
STATES—MOST OF TENNESSEE, PART OF ALABAMA,
KENTUCKY AND MISSISSIPPI, AND A SMALL BIT OF
GEORGIA, NORTH CAROLINA, AND VIRGINIA.

THE TVA STILL OPERATES TODAY.

Although voters and Congress approved of the New Deal, Franklin faced a big stumbling block with the Supreme Court. If a law passed by Congress goes against the Constitution, it is the Supreme Court's job to strike it down. It did just that with some of the "alphabet" programs, especially the AAA and the NRA. The court said the government did not have the right to start them or pay for them.

Franklin was furious. He had not appointed any of these judges to the Court. They were all conservative judges who believed in as little government as possible. Franklin wanted liberal judges who believed that it was the government's job to be involved. Besides, seven out of the nine judges were over seventy years old and appointed for life. He claimed they weren't getting enough work done fast enough. Franklin decided to pack the Court by appointing an additional judge for every judge over seventy.

To Franklin's surprise, Congress didn't like this idea at all. And neither did the people. Thousands of letters of protest came in. It was not often that Franklin lost a battle. But this time he did.

Over time he did get to choose seven judges. But his power had been checked.

# Chapter 7
# Living in the White House

"How do you like being president?" a reporter once asked Franklin.

"I love it!" he answered in a great, booming voice.

Franklin also liked living in the White House.

Eleanor wasn't so sure. She once told a friend, "I never wanted to be a president's wife." The First Lady had to host dinners for foreign visitors and parties for members of Congress and other people in government. She would stand for hours shaking hands.

Sometimes, however, Eleanor found being the First Lady fun. When the famous pilot Amelia Earhart came to town, she took

Eleanor flying. "It was like being on top of the world," Eleanor said.

Eleanor also traveled around the country for Franklin. He needed someone he could trust to see how his New Deal was working. He said that she was "his eyes and ears."

In West Virginia, she went down into a coal mine to talk to the miners.

When Sara heard about this, she wrote to Franklin. "I see she has emerged from the mine . . . That is something to be thankful for."

Traveling gave Eleanor a chance to speak about her own causes. She was a champion of the rights of African Americans and women. She urged Franklin to appoint more African Americans and women to government jobs—and he did.

Eleanor constantly wrote memos to Franklin about things she wanted him to do. They were put in a basket in his room each night. He'd read them before bed. The pile got so high that he told her she could only give him three memos a night.

Eleanor and Franklin were not the only Roosevelts living in the White House. It was home to their two youngest boys who were students at Groton. Their daughter, Anna, moved in with her children. So did their son James.

Louis Howe had the Lincoln bedroom. Missy LeHand, who had been Franklin's loyal secretary for thirteen years, also came.

Franklin's Scottie, Fala, was there, too, roaming the White House by day and sleeping in his bedroom at night.

Franklin's bedroom was on the second floor along with his private study where no one went without being asked. He kept his stamp collection on a desk near the door. Being president had its advantages. He asked the State Department to send him stamps on letters from other countries. Every Saturday, a package arrived at the White House.

FALA

Franklin woke around eight every morning.
He ate his breakfast and read the newspapers in
bed. Only his grandchildren were allowed in. He
didn't mind at all if they jumped on his bed. He
enjoyed it. Then he dressed and went over his

schedule with Louis Howe. At ten o'clock, he went down to his office. Each visitor was only supposed to stay around fifteen minutes. But Franklin loved to talk and he loved to listen. That's how he learned a lot. So he hardly ever kept to the schedule.

He had lunch around one. Depending on the day, he met with his cabinet or advisors. In the late afternoon he took care of letters and paperwork before going for a swim in the pool.

Then it was cocktail hour. He loved relaxing with family and friends. After dinner, he often worked on his stamp collection or watched a movie.

Franklin enjoyed meetings with reporters. On Wednesday mornings, he talked to reporters from the morning papers and, on Fridays afternoons, to reporters from the evening papers.

Reporters liked Franklin. He sat at his desk and they all crowded around filling up the Oval

Office. Sometimes a reporter would fall right onto his desk from all the pushing to get to the front. Unlike other presidents, he didn't ask to see questions beforehand. They could ask whatever they wanted. Sometimes he didn't want to answer. But he knew how to charm them so they didn't hold it against him.

# MARIAN ANDERSON SINGS

IN 1939, MARIAN ANDERSON, A FAMOUS AFRICAN-AMERICAN SINGER, WAS TO GIVE A CONCERT IN CONSTITUTION HALL, IN WASHINGTON, D.C. THE HALL WAS OWNED BY A WOMEN'S GROUP CALLED THE DAUGHTERS OF THE AMERICAN REVOLUTION (DAR). THEY REFUSED TO LET AN AFRICAN AMERICAN PERFORM THERE. ELEANOR HAD BEEN A MEMBER OF THE DAR. BUT NOW, NOT ONLY DID SHE RESIGN, SHE ALSO FOUND ANOTHER PLACE FOR MARIAN ANDERSON'S CONCERT—THE LINCOLN MEMORIAL.

ON EASTER SUNDAY AFTERNOON, SEVENTY-FIVE THOUSAND BLACKS AND WHITES CROWDED ALONG THE EDGE OF THE REFLECTION POOL TO HEAR MARIAN ANDERSON. MILLIONS MORE LISTENED FROM HOME ON THEIR RADIOS. MARIAN ANDERSON OPENED THE CONCERT WITH "AMERICA."

His life as president was exciting. Still, from the moment he took office, his goal had been to get people back to work. By the mid-1930s, times were getting better, but the county was not out of the Depression.

Then another problem—a big one—loomed across the Atlantic Ocean.

# Chapter 8
# Going to War

ADOLF HITLER

In 1933, Adolf Hitler had become chancellor of Germany. This was the same year that Franklin became president.

Hitler built up a mighty army. His aim was to conquer countries all over Europe. Germany would be the most powerful nation on earth.

In 1938, the German army rolled into Austria. During the next two years, Czechoslovakia, Poland, Norway, Denmark, the Netherlands, Belgium, Luxembourg, and finally France, fell to Germany. The people of Britain knew they could be next.

COUNTRIES UNDER GERMAN CONTROL BY 1940

America had sent troops to Europe to fight in World War I. Over 116,000 US soldiers had died. Americans didn't want to fight another war in Europe. In fact, Congress had passed laws to make sure America stayed out of wars between other countries. The US couldn't help any side; it couldn't even sell weapons. Still, Franklin knew that the US would probably become involved in the war one day. Germany might not attack America soon, but if it controlled all of Europe, it might.

Hitler was an enemy to be feared. Not only did he want to control the world, he wanted to get rid of what he considered inferior races, like Gypsies and Jews. Nazi death camps were set up in countries Hitler had invaded. Before the war ended, more than six million Jews were killed in these camps. As the war went on, other countries, including America, became aware of what was happening. But few acted. (It wasn't until 1944 that Franklin did anything to help rescue refugees.)

In 1940, Franklin's second term as president
was coming to an end. No president had ever run
for a third term. No one expected Franklin to.
But with the war in Europe, he felt he had to run

again. So he did. He didn't win by a landslide, but he won.

In July, Germany began bombing Britain. Every night fires raged all over London. Every day military bases were hit hard. Young British pilots fought bravely, even though they were outnumbered. The prime minister, Winston Churchill, begged Franklin for help. Churchill understood that America could not enter the war. But Churchill badly needed destroyers.

"Mr. President," he pleaded, "with great respect, I must tell you that in the long history of the world, this is the thing to do now."

Franklin wanted to send destroyers. But Britain couldn't pay for them. So Franklin's hands were tied. Then, together, he and Churchill came up with a plan.

America would loan Britain fifty destroyers. In return, Britain would allow America to have some military bases on British territory near the United States for ninety-nine years. This led to Congress approving the Lend-Lease Act. Finally, America could send badly needed war supplies to Britain. Convoys of ships went back and forth, often under attack from German subs.

Franklin not only had to worry about Germany, but he had to worry about her allies, Italy and, especially, Japan.

Japan had a strong military. The Japanese had been fighting in China for years. Now they had their eye on other countries in Asia such as Indochina and the Philippines.

Franklin was sure that one day Japan would attack the United States. But where and when it happened came as a horrible surprise.

On Sunday, December 7, 1941, Japanese warplanes attacked Pearl Harbor in the US territory of Hawaii. In fifteen minutes, the Japanese bombed the airfields and smashed battleships. Over thirty-five hundred Americans were killed or wounded. Two hundred and sixty-five planes were destroyed. Nine ships were damaged or sunk. Among them was the USS *Arizona*, the battleship Franklin had watched being built in Brooklyn during World War I.

The next day, Americans gathered around their radios to hear the president speak about the attack. He said that December 7, 1941, was "a date which will live in infamy." The United States declared war on Japan that same day. Three days later, Germany and Italy declared war on America. The United States was now part of World War II.

Men over eighteen joined the army and navy. Almost overnight, factories that had been building items like toys and cars were turning out weapons, trucks, tanks, and planes. Women worked

 alongside men. Pictures of "Rosie the Riveter" became the symbol of women helping the war effort. No one was out of work now.

"It will not only be a long war, it will be a hard war," Franklin told the country. But he added, "We are going to win the war and we are going to win the peace that follows."

The war was raging on three fronts—in Europe, North Africa, and the Pacific.

# FRANKLIN AND WINSTON

ON AUGUST 9, 1941, IN THE WATERS OFF
NEWFOUNDLAND IN CANADA, WINSTON CHURCHILL
AND FRANKLIN ROOSEVELT MET FOR THE FIRST
TIME. THAT SUNDAY, BEFORE GOING HOME, THE
TWO LEADERS TOOK PART IN A MOVING SERVICE
ABOARD *THE PRINCE OF WALES*, A BRITISH
BATTLESHIP. SAILORS AND MARINES FROM
AMERICA AND BRITAIN STOOD SIDE BY SIDE
SINGING HYMNS AS THE PRESIDENT AND THE
PRIME MINISTER SAT TOGETHER.

IT WAS THE BEGINNING OF A WONDERFUL
FRIENDSHIP BETWEEN TWO GIANTS OF THEIR
GENERATION. DURING THE WAR, THEY WOULD
MEET ELEVEN MORE TIMES, IN EUROPE AND IN
NORTH AMERICA.

A breakthrough came in the Pacific on June 4, 1942, at the Battle of Midway. The Americans had broken the Japanese's secret codes, so they knew about the attack and were ready. The battle went on for four days. When it was over, the Americans had sunk all four Japanese carriers.

Finally, the US Navy had a victory. Japan never took control of the seas again. Still, a long struggle to victory lay ahead as brave soldiers fought fierce battles on Okinawa, Iwo Jima, and other Japanese islands.

# JAPANESE CAMPS

AFTER PEARL HARBOR, FEAR SPREAD THAT THE JAPANESE MIGHT ATTACK THE MAINLAND. THAT NEVER HAPPENED, BUT PEOPLE WERE PANICKED. MOST OF THE JAPANESE AMERICANS IN THE UNITED STATES LIVED ON THE WEST COAST. WHAT IF SOME OF THEM WERE SPIES?

IN FEBRUARY 1942, FRANKLIN SIGNED AN ORDER WHICH FORCED JAPANESE AMERICANS ON THE WEST COAST TO SPEND THE WAR IN ARMED CAMPS SURROUNDED BY BARBED WIRE. ABOUT ONE HUNDRED AND TEN THOUSAND PEOPLE HAD TO LEAVE THEIR HOMES AND TAKE WITH THEM ONLY WHAT THEY COULD CARRY. MEN, WOMEN, CHILDREN,

AND ELDERLY PEOPLE ALL HAD TO GO. IT WAS A TERRIBLE THING TO DO.

NONE WERE CONVICTED AS SPIES AND ABOUT TWENTY THOUSAND JAPANESE-AMERICAN YOUNG MEN JOINED THE US ARMY AND FOUGHT BRAVELY IN NORTH AFRICA AND EUROPE.

WHEN THE WAR WAS OVER, PEOPLE WERE LET GO WITH $25 AND A TRAIN TICKET. MOST HAD LOST THEIR HOMES, THEIR FARMS, AND THEIR BUSINESSES. FINALLY, AFTER MANY YEARS, EACH DETAINEE OR THEIR HEIR WAS GIVEN $20,000 BY THE GOVERNMENT.

The invasion of Europe took place on June 6, 1944. It became known as D-day. Nearly five thousand ships ferried over one hundred thousand men across the English Channel to the beaches at Normandy in France. They met heavy fire from the Germans and Allied losses were staggering. But they held their beachhead and, within two weeks, close to six hundred thousand soldiers and equipment had landed at Normandy. It was an unbelievable accomplishment.

Eleven months later, on May 7, 1945, Germany would surrender.

# Chapter 9
# Saying Good-Bye

At home in 1944, it was time for a presidential election. Not only was Franklin running the war

HARRY S. TRUMAN

as Commander-in-Chief, now he was running for a fourth term as president. Senator Harry S. Truman from Missouri was his running mate.

Franklin was tired. Still, he campaigned with the same confidence, charm, and good humor. He told crowds that his opponents now were attacking his little dog, Fala. With a straight face, he said, "Well, of course, I don't resent attacks, and my family doesn't resent attacks, but Fala does resent attacks." Everyone burst out laughing.

It came as no surprise when Franklin won

again. After all, America was in a war and many people felt that it was no time to change presidents.

In January 1945, Franklin traveled to Yalta on the Black Sea to meet with Churchill and Joseph Stalin, the Russian leader. Franklin's goal was to get a promise from Stalin that Russia would help fight Japan. And he wanted Stalin to agree that Russia would be part of a world peace organization after the war. It would become the United Nations.

Franklin returned home with Stalin's promises, looking tired and drawn. He had dark circles under his eyes and he had lost weight. Eleanor was worried about him.

He told Congress about the trip to Yalta. For the first time, he did not stand when he spoke. "I hope you will pardon me for . . . sitting down . . .

but I know that you will realize that it makes it a lot easier for me in not having to carry about ten pounds of steel around on the bottom of my legs, and also because of the fact that I have just completed a fourteen-thousand-mile trip."

Soon after, Franklin went to Warm Springs for a much needed rest. Eleanor stayed in Washington, but friends traveled down with him. After the first week, he looked better and was enjoying the company.

On April 12, he woke up with a headache and a stiff neck. He ate breakfast, dressed, and joined friends. His cousin remembered him looking particularly handsome in a gray suit and crimson tie.

Just before lunch, he was sitting at a table going over the mail. Suddenly he said he had a terrific headache and slumped down.

A doctor was called, but it was too late. A little before 3:30 PM, Franklin Roosevelt died of a burst blood vessel in his brain. He was sixty-three years old. Not just the country, but the whole world was stunned by the news.

Eleanor came down from Washington to take her husband home. The railroad station at Warm Springs was packed with friends and neighbors who had come to say good-bye to their old friend.

As the train wound its way to Washington, crowds of people stood along the tracks, weeping. A reporter wrote, "They came from the fields and the farms, from hamlets and crossroads and in the cities they thronged by the thousands to stare with humble reverence and awe."

In the morning, the train arrived in
Washington, D.C. A caisson, drawn by six white
horses, carried Franklin's coffin to the White
House. There was a funeral in the East Room
that afternoon. In the evening, the train
continued up along the Hudson River to Hyde

Park where Franklin was buried at home at
Springwood the next day.

"The funeral was very beautiful," a friend
wrote. "The day was gloriously snappy, very
sunny and blue, white lilacs were in bloom . . .
and the birds were singing."

Harry S. Truman was now president. Less than a month later, on May 7, 1945, Germany surrendered. In August, Truman gave orders to drop atomic bombs on two cities in Japan—Hiroshima and Nagasaki. (Scientists had been secretly working on the atomic bomb since 1941.) Japan surrendered on September 2, 1945.

World War II was finally over.

Soon after Franklin's death, a young soldier said what so many Americans felt about him. "I can remember the president ever since I was a little kid . . . America will seem a strange empty place without his voice talking to the people whenever great events occur . . . I can hardly believe he is gone."

Many terrible events occurred while Franklin was in office. Yet, with him, Americans felt as if they always had a friend helping them through the hard times.

# TIMELINE OF
# FRANKLIN ROOSEVELT'S LIFE

| | |
|---|---|
| 1882 | Born in Hyde Park, New York, on January 30 |
| 1900 | Graduates from Groton School, a boarding school in Massachusetts |
| 1903 | Graduates from Harvard with a B.A. in History |
| 1905 | Marries his distant cousin Eleanor Roosevelt on March 17 Anna Eleanor, the first of their six children, is born |
| 1910 | Runs for the New York State Senate and wins |
| 1913 | Becomes Assistant Secretary of the Navy |
| 1919 | Attends peace conference in France, formally ending World War I |
| 1920 | Runs for vice president on a ticket with James Cox |
| 1921 | Contracts polio |
| 1924 | Visits Warm Springs, Georgia, for the first time |
| 1928 | Elected governor of New York |
| 1932 | Elected president of the United States |
| 1933 | Gives first "fireside chat" on the radio |
| 1936 | Reelected president for second term |
| 1940 | Reelected president for third term |
| 1941 | Asks Congress to declare war on Japan |
| 1944 | Reelected president for fourth term |
| 1945 | Dies in Warm Springs, Georgia, on April 12 |

# TIMELINE OF
# THE WORLD

Thomas Edision brings electric light to one square mile in — **1882**
New York City

First Klondike Gold Rush begins in Yukon, Canada — **1896**

First World Series is played between Boston and — **1903**
Pittsburgh

Henry Ford's Model T car popularizes automobiles — **1908**

*Titanic* sinks on its maiden voyage between Great Britain — **1912**
and America on April 14

World War I — **1914–1918**

Russian Revolution begins — **1917**

Nineteenth Amendment gives US women the right to vote — **1920**

Adolph Hitler becomes the leader of the Nazi Party in — **1921**
Germany

Hormone insulin is discovered and used to treat diabetes — **1922**

Charles Lindbergh flies the first nonstop, solo, transatlantic — **1927**
flight between America and France

Stock market on Wall Street crashes — **1929**

African-American Jesse Owens wins four gold medals at — **1936**
the Summer Olympics in Berlin, Germany

Amelia Earhart's plane disappears over the Pacific Ocean — **1937**

Action Comics publishes the first Superman comic book — **1938**

Germany invades Poland and World War II begins — **1939**

Japan bombs Pearl Harbor, Hawaii — **1941**
United States enters World War II

Largest concentration camp in Auschwitz, Germany, is — **1945**
liberated by the Soviet Army

# BIBLIOGRAPHY

The starred books are for young readers.

Brands. H. W. **Traitor to His Class: The Privileged Life and Radical Presidency of Franklin Delano Roosevelt**. Doubleday, New York, 2008.

*Freedman, Russell. **Franklin Delano Roosevelt**. Clarion Books, New York, 1990.

Goodwin, Doris Kearns. **No Ordinary Time: Franklin & Eleanor: The Home Front in World War II**. Simon & Schuster, New York. 1995.

*Sullivan, Wilson. **American Heritage Junior Library: Franklin Delano Roosevelt**. American Heritage Publishing Co., Inc., 1970.

*Thompson, Gare. **Who Was Eleanor Roosevelt?** Grosset & Dunlap, New York. 2004.

*Waxman, Laura Hamilton. **Franklin D. Roosevelt**. Barnes & Noble, New York. 2004.